Photographer • Jarek Duk
Art Direction & Stylist • Georgina Brant
Hair & Make Up • Lauren Palmer
Design Layout • Lindsay Birch for Quail Studio
Model • Amy Neville (BMA Model Management)

First published in Great Britain in 2019 by
Quail Publishing Limited
Old Town Hall, Market Square, Buckingham, Buckinghamshire,
MK18 1NJ
E-mail: info@quailstudio.co.uk

ISBN: 978-0-9935908-8-7

essential
sweaters

8 cosy hand knit designs
to compliment your style

quail studio

contents

introduction

Essential Sweaters is a collection of 8 sweater designs from the Quail Studio team.

The collection features timeless designs with small details. All styled with everyday wearable fashion pieces, the designs feature Rowan's core yarns and our signature Quail Studio style.

Whether it is the oversized roll neck collar sweater (Luna) or the throw-on 'poncho style' sweater (Amber), we have designed the collection to be easy to wear and stylish at the same time.

We have focused our design attention in this collection to really focus on the fit and shape of the designs, ensuring that after you have hand knitted your piece, it is comfortable and gives you the look that you were hoping for.

Taking inspiration from high street fashion trends, and pairing designs with a simple and refined colour palette, *Essential Sweaters* is a collection that bridges the gap between our oversized designs and our more fitted fashion pieces.

q u a i l   s t u d i o

gallery

Luna *pg 28*

Maple *pg 30*

Breeze *pg 34*

Orla *pg 38*

Bramble pg 42

Clover pg 46

Maize pg 50

Amber pg 54

9

Luna
Rowan Felted Tweed Aran
pg 28

Maple
Rowan Alpaca Classic pg 30

Breeze
Rowan Kid Classic
pg 34

Orla

Rowan Alpaca Soft DK pg 38

Bramble
Rowan Brushed Fleece pg 42

Clover

Rowan Cocoon pg 46

Maize

Rowan Cashmere Tweed pg 50

Amber

Rowan Felted Tweed pg 54

the patterns

SIZE SCHEMATIC

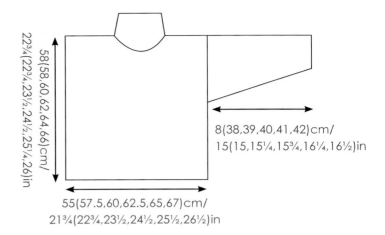

8(38,39,40,41,42)cm/
15(15,15¼,15¾,16¼,16½)in

22¾(22¾,23½,24,24½,25¼,26)in / 58(58,60,62,64,66)cm

55(57.5,60,62.5,65,67)cm/
21¾(22¾,23½,24½,25½,26½)in

Luna

SIZES
To Fit Bust

71 – 76	81 – 86	91 – 97	102 – 107	112 – 117	122 – 127	cm
28 – 30	32 – 34	36 – 38	40 – 42	44 – 46	48 – 50	in

Actual Size

110	115	120	125	130	134	cm
43¼	45¼	47¼	49¼	51¼	52¾	in

YARN
Rowan Felted Tweed Aran
13(14,15,16,16,17) x 50g balls of Rowan Felted Tweed Aran (photographed in Scree)

NEEDLES
5mm (no 6) (US 8) needles

TENSION
16 stitches and 28 rows to 10cm/4in measured over garter stitch using 5mm (US 8) needles.
16 stitches and 23 rows to 10cm/4in measured over stocking stitch using 5mm (US 8) needles.

EXTRAS
Stitch markers
Stitch holders

FRONT
Using 5mm (US 8) needles, cast on 86(90,94,98,102,106) sts.

Row 1 (RS): K2, *P2, K2, rep from * to end.
Row 2 (WS): P2, *K2, P2, rep from * to end.
Rows 1 and 2 form rib patt.

Cont straight in rib patt until front meas 3cm/1¼in, ending with WS row and inc 2 sts evenly along last row. 88[92,96,100,104,108] sts.

Work straight in g st until front meas 38(38,39,40,41,42)cm/15(15,15½,15¾,16¼,16½)in, ending with a WS row.
Mark each end of last row.

Cont in g st until front meas 18(18,19,20,21,22)cm /7(7,7½,8,8¼,8¾)in from markers, ending with a WS row.

Shape neck
Next row (RS): K34(36,37,39,40,42), turn, leaving rem sts on a stitch holder. 34[36,37,39,40,42] sts.

Next row (WS): Cast off 4 sts, K to end. 30[32,33,35,36,38] sts.
Next row (RS): Knit.
Rep last 2 rows twice more. 22[24,25,27,28,30] sts.

Shape shoulders
Cast off.

With RS facing, slip centre 20(20,22,22,24,24) sts onto a stitch holder, rejoin yarn to rem 34(36,37,39,40,42) sts and K to end. 34[36,37,39,40,42] sts.

Next row (WS): Knit.
Next row (RS): Cast off 4, K to end. 30[32,33,35,36,38] sts.
Rep last 2 rows twice more. 22[24,25,27,28,30] sts.

Shape shoulders
Cast off.

BACK
Using 5mm (US 8) needles, cast on 86(90,94,98,102,106) sts.

Work straight in rib patt as for front until back meas 3cm/1¼in, ending with a WS row and inc 2 sts evenly along last row. 88[92,96,100,104,108] sts.

Work straight in g st until back meas 38(38,39,40,41,42)cm/15(15,15½,15¾,16¼,16½)in, ending with a WS row.

Mark each end of last row.

Cont in g st until back meas same as front to start of shoulder shaping, ending with a WS row.

Shape shoulders
Cont in g st, cast off 22(24,25,27,28,30) at beg of next 2 rows. 44[44,46,46,48,48] sts.
Slip rem sts onto a stitch holder.

SLEEVES (make two)
Using 5mm (US 8) needles, cast on 38(38,42,42,42,46) sts.

Work straight in rib patt as for front until work meas 3cm/1¼in, ending with a WS row.

Starting with a K row, work in st st for 4 rows.

Next row (RS): K2, M1, K to last 2 sts, M1, K2. 40[40,44,44,44,48] sts.

Cont in st st, working inc as set above, inc 1 st at each end of 7(7,6,8,13,9) foll 4th rows, then on 5(5,6,5,2,5) foll 6th rows. 64[64,68,70,74,76] sts.

Cont straight in st st until sleeve meas 32(32,33,34,35,36)cm/12½(12½,13,13½,13¾,14¼)in, ending with a WS row.
Work in g st until sleeve meas 38(38,39,40,41,42)cm/15(15,15½,15¾,16¼,16½)in, ending with a WS row.

Cast off.

MAKING UP
Press as described on the information page.
Join right shoulder seam using mattress stitch.

ROLL NECKBAND
With RS facing and using 5mm (US 8) needles, pick up and knit 14(14,15,15,16,16) sts down left front neck, knit 20(20,22,22,24,24) sts from front neck stitch holder, pick up and knit 14(14,15,15,16,16) sts up right front neck, knit 44(44,46,46,48,48) sts from back neck stitch holder. 92[92,98,98,104,104] sts.

Next row (WS): P2, *Kfb, P2, rep from * to end. 122[122,130,130,138,138] sts.

Work straight in rib as for front until roll neck meas 35cm/13¾in, ending with a WS row.
Cast off loosely in rib.

Join left shoulder and roll neckband seams, reversing neckband seam 5cm/2in up from neck edge.
Sew cast-off edge of sleeve between markers on side edges of back and front.
Join side and sleeve seams.

SIZE SCHEMATIC

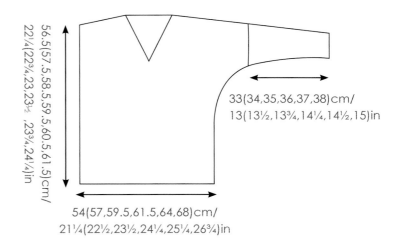

56.5(57.5,58.5,59.5,60.5,61.5)cm/
22¼(22¾,23,23½,23¾,24¼)in

33(34,35,36,37,38)cm/
13(13½,13¾,14¼,14½,15)in

54(57,59.5,61.5,64,68)cm/
21¼(22½,23½,24¼,25¼,26¾)in

Maple

SIZES

To Fit Bust

71 – 76	81 – 86	91 – 97	102 – 107	112 – 117	122 – 127	cm
28 – 30	32 – 34	36 – 38	40 – 42	44 – 46	48 – 50	in

Actual Size

108	114	119	123	128	136	cm
42½	45	46¾	48½	50½	53¼	in

YARN

Rowan Alpaca Classic
15(16,16,17,17,18) x 25g balls of Rowan Alpaca
Classic (photographed in shade Soft Satin 116)

NEEDLES

4.5mm (no 7) (US 7) needles

TENSION

19 stitches and 26 rows to 10cm/4in measured
over stocking stitch using 4.5mm (US 7) needles
and holding 2 strands of Rowan Alpaca Classic
yarn held together.
25 stitches and 29 rows to 10cm/4in measured
over rib using 4.5mm (US 7) needles and holding
2 strands of Rowan Alpaca Classic yarn held
together.

EXTRAS

Stitch markers
Stitch holders

FRONT

Using 4.5mm (US 7) needles and 2 strands of
Rowan Alpaca Classic yarn held together
throughout, cast on 102(107,112,117,122,127) sts.

Row 1 (RS): P2, *K3, P2, rep from * to end.
Row 2 (WS): K2, *P3, K2, rep from * to end.
Rows 1 and 2 form rib patt.

Cont straight in rib patt until front meas 4cm/1½in,
ending with a WS row and inc 1(2,1,0,1,2) sts
evenly along last row. 103[109,113,117,123,129] sts.

Starting with a K row, work in st st until front meas
33cm/13in, ending with a WS row.

Shape for sleeves
Cont in st st, cast on 2 sts at beg of next 4 rows.
111[117,121,125,131,137] sts.
Cast on 3 sts at beg of next 4 rows.
123[129,133,137,143,149] sts.
Cast on 4 sts at beg of next 4 rows.
139[145,149,153,159,165] sts.
Mark each end of last row.

Cont straight in st st until front meas 4(5,6,6,7,8)cm /1½(2,2¼,2¼,2¾,3¼)in from markers, ending with a WS row.

Shape neck
Next row (RS): K70(73,75,77,80,83), turn, leaving rem sts on a stitch holder. 70[73,75,77,80,83] sts.
Next row (WS): Purl.

Next row (RS): K to last 4 sts, K2tog, K2.
69[72,74,76,79,82] sts.
Next row (WS): Purl.
Rep last 2 rows 13(13,13,14,14,14) times more.
56[59,61,62,65,68] sts.

Shape shoulder
Next row (RS): Cast off 9(9,10,10,10,11), K to last 4 sts, K2tog, K2. 46[49,50,51,54,56] sts.
Next row (WS): Purl.
Rep last 2 rows 1(2,2,2,2,2) times more.
36[29,28,29,32,32] sts.

Next row (RS): Cast off 9(9,10,10,10,11), K to end.
27[20,18,19,22,21] sts.
Next row (WS): Purl.
Rep last 2 rows 1(0,0,0,0,0) times more.
18[20,18,19,22,21] sts.

Next row (RS): Cast off 9(10,9,10,11,11), K to end.
9[10,9,9,11,10] sts.
Next row (WS): Purl.

Cast off.

With RS facing, rejoin yarn to rem 69(72,74,76,79,82) sts, cast on 1 st, K to end.
70[73,75,77,80,83] sts.

Next row (WS): Purl.
Next row (RS): K2, Sl 1, K1, psso, K to end.
69[72,74,76,79,82] sts.
Rep last 2 rows 14(14,14,15,15,15) times more.
55[58,60,61,64,67] sts.

Shape shoulder
Next row (WS): Cast off 9(9,10,10,10,11), P to end.
46[49,50,51,54,56] sts.
Next row (RS): K2, Sl 1, K1, psso, K to end.
45[48,49,50,53,55] sts.
Rep last 2 rows 0(1,1,1,1,1) time more.
45[38,38,39,42,43] sts.

Next row (WS): Cast off 9(9,10,10,10,11), P to end.
36[29,28,29,32,32] sts.
Next row (RS): Knit.
Rep last 2 rows 2(1,1,1,1,1) times more.
18[20,18,19,22,21] sts.

Next row (WS): Cast off 9(10,9,10,11,11), P to end.
9[10,9,9,11,10] sts.
Next row (RS): Knit.

Cast off.

BACK
Using 4.5mm (US 7) needles and 2 strands of Rowan Alpaca Classic yarn held together throughout, cast on 102(107,112,117,122,127) sts.

Work straight in rib patt as for front until back meas 4cm/1½in, ending with a WS row and inc 1(2,1,0,1,2) sts evenly along last row.
103[109,113,117,123,129] sts.

Starting with a K row, work in st st until back meas 33cm/13in, ending with a WS row.

Shape for sleeves
Cont in st st, cast on 2 sts at beg of next 4 rows.
111[117,121,125,131,137] sts.
Cast on 3 sts at beg of next 4 rows.
123[129,133,137,143,149] sts.
Cast on 4 sts at beg of next 4 rows.
139[145,149,153,159,165] sts.
Mark each end of last row.

Cont straight in st st until back meas same as front to start of shoulder shaping, ending with a WS row.

Shape shoulders
Cont in st st, cast off 9(9,10,10,10,11) at beg of next 8(8,8,10,8,10) rows. 67[73,69,53,79,55] sts.
Cast off 9(10,9,9,11,10) at beg of next 4(4,4,2,4,2) rows. 31[33,33,35,35,35] sts.

Cast off.

SLEEVES (make two)

Using 4.5mm (US 7) needles and 2 strands of Rowan Alpaca Classic yarn held together throughout, cast on 48(48,53,53,58,58) sts.

Row 1 (RS): K3, *P2, K3, rep from * to end.
Row 2 (WS): P3, *K2, P3, rep from * to end.
Rows 1 and 2 form rib patt.

Cont straight in rib patt until sleeve meas 6cm/2¼in, ending with a WS row.

Next row (RS): P in front and K in back of first st, K2, *P2, K3, rep from * to last 5 sts, P2, K2, K in front and P in back of last st. 50[50,55,55,60,50] sts.
Next row (WS): K1, P3, *K2, P3, rep from * to last st, K1.
Next row: P1, K3, *P2, K3, rep from * to last st, P1.
Next row: K1, P3, *K2, P3, rep from * to last st, K1.

Next row (RS): P in front and back of first st, K3, *P2, K3, rep from * to last st, P in front and back of last st. 52[52,57,57,62,62] sts.
Next row (WS): K2, *P3, K2, rep from * to end.
Next row: P2, *K3, P2, rep from * to end.
Next row: K2, *P3, K2, rep from * to end.

Next row (RS): K in front and P in back of first st, P1, *K3, P2, rep from * to last 5 sts, K3, P1, P in front and K in back of last st. 54[54,59,59,64,64] sts.
Next row (WS): P1, K2, *P3, K2, rep from * to last st, P1.
Next row: K1, P2, *K3, P2, rep from * to last st, K1.
Next row: P1, K2, *P3, K2, rep from * to last st, P1.

Next row (RS): K in front and back of first st, P2, *K3, P2, rep from * to last st, K in front and back of last st. 56[56,61,61,66,66] sts.
Next row (WS): P2, *K2, P3, rep from * to last 4 sts, K2, P2.
Next row: K2, *P2, K3, rep from * to last 4 sts, P2, K2.
Next row: P2, *K2, P3, rep from * to last 4 sts, K2, P2.

Next row (RS): K in front and back of first st, K1, P2, *K3, P2, rep from * to last 2 sts, K1, K in front and back of last st. 58[58,63,63,68,68] sts.
Next row (WS): P3, *K2, P3, rep from * to end.
Next row: K3, *P2, K3, rep from * to end.
Next row: P3, *K2, P3, rep from * to end.

Cont increasing as set to maintain rib patt, inc 1 st at each end of next row and 8(10,10,13,13,15) following 4th rows. 76[80,85,91,96,100] sts.

Cont straight in rib until sleeve meas 33(34,35,36,37,38)cm/13(13½,13¾,14¼,14½,15)in, ending with a WS row.

Cast off loosely in rib.

MAKING UP

Press as described on the information page.
Join shoulder seams using mattress stitch.
Sew cast-off edge of sleeve between markers on side edges of back and front.
Join side and sleeve seams.
Catch down cast-on st at centre of front neck on WS.

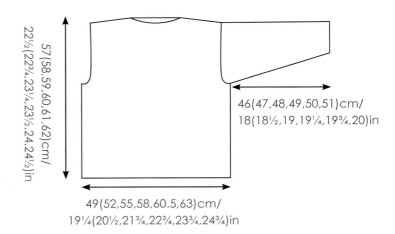

57(58,59,60,61,62)cm/
22½(22¾,23¼,23½,24,24½)in

46(47,48,49,50,51)cm/
18(18½,19,19¼,19¾,20)in

49(52,55,58,60.5,63)cm/
19¼(20½,21¾,22¾,23¾,24¾)in

Breeze

SIZES

To Fit Bust

71 – 76	81 – 86	91 – 97	102 – 107	112 – 117	122 – 127	cm
28 – 30	32 – 34	36 – 38	40 – 42	44 – 46	48 – 50	in

Actual Size

98	104	110	116	121	126	cm
38½	41	43¼	45¾	47¾	49½	in

YARN

Rowan Kid Classic
10(11,11,12,12,13) x 50g balls of Rowan Kid Classic
(photographed in shade Drought 876)

NEEDLES

4.5mm (no 7) (US 7) and 5mm (no 6) (US 8) needles

TENSION

28 stitches and 26 rows to 10cm/4in measured
over patt using 5mm (US 8) needles.

EXTRAS

Cable needle
Stitch holders

SPECIAL ABBREVIATIONS

C8F – slip next 4 sts onto cable needle and hold at
front of work, K4, then K4 from cable needle.
C8B – slip next 4 sts onto cable needle and hold at
back of work, K4, then K4 from cable needle.

BACK

Using 4.5mm (US 7) needles, cast on
104(110,119,125,131,140) sts.
Next row (RS): K2, *P1, K2, rep from * to end.
Next row (WS): P2, *K1, P2, rep from * to end.
Rep last 2 rows of rib until back meas 6cm/2½in,
ending with a WS row.

Change to 5mm (US 8) needles.

Next row (RS): K2(2,8,8,8,14), *Kfb, K2, rep from
* to last 3(3,9,9,9,15) sts, Kfb, K2(2,8,8,8,14).
138(146,154,162,170,178) sts.

Row 1 (WS): Purl.
Row 2 (RS): K9(1,9,1,9,1), *C8B, K8, rep from * to last
st, K1.
Row 3: Purl.
Row 4: Knit.
Row 5: Purl.

Row 6: K1(9,1,9,1,9), *C8F, K8, rep from * to last 9 sts, * C8F, K1.
Row 7: Purl.
Row 8: Knit.
Rows 1 to 8 form patt.

Cont in patt until back meas 34(34,35,35,35,35) cm/13½(13½,13¾,13¾,13¾,13¾)in, ending with a WS row.

Shape armholes
Cast off 4 sts at beg of next 2 rows.
130[138,146,154,162,170] sts.

Next row (RS): Sl 1, K1, psso, patt to last 2 sts, K2tog.
128[136,144,152,160,168] sts.
Next row (WS): P2tog, patt to last 2 sts, P2tog.
126[134,142,150,158,166] sts.
Rep last 2 rows once more.
122[130,138,146,154,162] sts.

Cont straight in patt until back meas 23(24,24,25,26,27)cm/9(9½,9½,10,10¼,10½)in from start of armhole shaping, ending with a WS row.

Shape shoulders
Next row (RS): Cast off 38(42,46,48,52,56) sts, patt to last 38(42,46,48,52,56), cast off last 38(42,46,48,52,56) sts. 46[46,46,50,50,50] sts.

Slip rem sts onto a stitch holder.

FRONT
Using 4.5mm (US 7) needles, cast on 104(110,119,125,131,140) sts.
Work in rib as for back until front meas 6cm/2½in, ending with a WS row.

Change to 5mm (US 8) needles.

Next row (RS): K2(2,8,8,8,14), *Kfb, K2, rep from * to last 3(3,9,9,9,15) sts, Kfb, K2(2,8,8,8,14). 138(146,154,162,170,178) sts.

Work straight in patt as for back until front meas 34(34,35,35,35,35)cm/13½(13½,13¾,13¾,13¾,13¾)in, ending with a WS row.

Shape armholes
Cast off 4 sts at beg of next 2 rows.
130[138,146,154,162,170] sts.

Next row (RS): Sl 1, K1, psso, patt to last 2 sts, K2tog.
128[136,144,152,160,168] sts.
Next row (WS): P2tog, patt to last 2 sts, P2tog.

126[134,142,150,158,166] sts.
Rep last 2 rows once more.
122[130,138,146,154,162] sts.

Cont straight in patt until front meas 18(19,19,19,20,21)cm/7(7½,7½,7½,8,8¼)in from start of armhole shaping, ending with a WS row.

Shape neck
Next row (RS): Patt 46(50,54,56,60,64), turn, leaving rem sts on a stitch holder.

Next row (WS): P2tog, patt to end.
45[49,53,55,59,63] sts.
Next row (RS): Patt to last 2 sts, K2tog.
44[48,52,54,58,62] sts.
Rep last 2 row 3 times more. 38[42,46,48,52,56] sts.

Cont straight in patt until front meas same as back to start of shoulder shaping, ending with a WS row.

Shape shoulder
Cast off rem 38(42,46,48,52,56) sts.

With RS facing, slip centre 30(30,30,34,34,34) sts onto a stitch holder, rejoin yarn to rem 46(50,54,56,60,64) sts and patt to end.

Next row (WS): Patt to last 2 sts, P2togtbl.
45[49,53,55,59,63] sts.
Next row (RS): Sl 1, K1, psso, patt to end.
44[48,52,54,58,62] sts.
Rep last 2 rows 3 times more. 38[42,46,48,52,56] sts.

Cont straight in patt until front meas same as back to start of shoulder shaping, ending with a WS row.

Shape shoulder
Cast off rem 38(42,46,48,52,56) sts.

SLEEVES (make two)
Using 4.5mm (US 7) needles, cast on 65(71,74,77,83,83) sts.
Work in rib as for back until sleeve meas 6cm/2½in, ending with a WS row.

Change to 5mm (US 8) needles.

Next row (RS): K8(8,2,8,8,8), *Kfb, K2, rep from * to last 9(9,3,9,9,9) sts, Kfb, K to end.
82[90,98,98,106,106] sts.

Row 1 (WS): Purl.
Row 2 (RS): K1(9,1,1,9,9), *C8B, K8, rep from * to last 17 sts, C8B, K9.

Row 3: Purl.
Row 4: Knit.
Row 5: Purl.
Row 6: K9(1,9,9,1,1), *C8F, K8, * to last 9 sts, C8F, K1.
Row 7: Purl.
Row 8: Knit.
Rows 1 to 8 form patt.

Next row (WS): Kfb, patt to last st, Kfb.
84[92,100,100,108,108] sts.

Cont in patt, working inc as set above, inc 1 st at each end of 7(5,2,2,3,6) foll 4th (4th,8th,6th,8th,4th) rows and 7(8,7,10,7,7) foll 8th(8th,10th,8th,10th,10th) rows, incorporating increased sts into st st. 112[118,118,124,128,134] sts.

Cont straight in patt until sleeve meas 46(47,48,49,50,51)cm/18(18½,19,19¼,19¾,20)in, ending with a WS row.

Shape sleeve top
Cont in patt, cast off 4 sts at beg of next 2 rows. 104[110,110,116,120,126] sts.

Next row (RS): Sl 1, K1, psso, patt to last 2 sts, K2tog. 102[108,108,114,118,124] sts.
Next row (WS): Purl.
Rep last 2 rows once more. 100[106,106,112,116,122] sts.

Cont in patt, cast off 10(11,11,11,12,13) sts at beg of next 6 rows. 40[40,40,46,44,44] sts.

Cast off.

MAKING UP
Press as described on the information page.
Join right shoulder seam using mattress stitch.

NECKBAND
With RS facing and using 4.5mm (US 7) needles, pick up and knit 13(13,13,15,15,15) sts down left front neck, work across sts from front neck stitch holder as follows: K1(1,1,3,3,3),*K2tog, K3, rep from * 4 times more, K2tog, K2(2,2,4,4,4), then pick up and knit 12(12,12,14,14,14) sts up right front neck, work across sts from back neck stitch holder as follows: K2(2,2,4,4,4),*K2tog, K3, rep from * 7 times more, K2tog, K2(2,2,4,4,4). 86[86,86,98,98,98] sts.

Next row (WS): P2, *K1, P2, rep from * to end.
Next row (RS): K2, *P1, K2, rep from * to end.
Rep last 2 rows of rib until neckband meas

4cm/1½in, ending with a WS row.

Cast off in rib.

Join left shoulder and neckband seams.
Sew in sleeves.
Join side and sleeve seams.

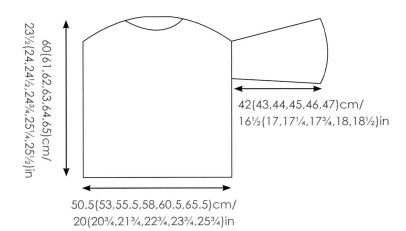

SIZE SCHEMATIC

23½(24,24,24½,24¾,25¼,25½)in
60(61,62,63,64,65)cm/

42(43,44,45,46,47)cm/
16½(17,17¼,17¾,18,18½)in

50.5(53,55.5,58,60.5,65.5)cm/
20(20¾,21¾,22¾,23¾,25¾)in

Orla

SIZES
To Fit Bust

71 – 76	81 – 86	91 – 97	102 – 107	112 – 117	122 – 127	cm
28 – 30	32 – 34	36 – 38	40 – 42	44 – 46	48 – 50	in

Actual Size

101	106	110	116	121	131	cm
39¾	41¾	43¼	45¾	47¾	51½	in

YARN
Rowan Alpaca Soft DK
12(12,13,14,14,15) x 50g balls of Rowan Alpaca Soft DK (photographed in shade Rainy Day 210)

NEEDLES
4mm (no 8) (US 6) needles

TENSION
16 stitches and 22 rows to 10cm/4in measured over pattern using 4mm (US 6) needles.

EXTRAS
Stitch holders
Stitch markers

PATTERN NOTE
When working in patt, the YO above slipped stitch is not counted as a stitch throughout.

BACK
Using 4mm (US 6) needles, cast on 81(85,89,93,97,105) sts.

Next row (WS): K1, *YO, Sl 1, K1, rep from * to end.

Row 1 (RS): K1, *K next st tog with YO of previous row, YO, Sl 1, rep from * to last 2 sts, K next st tog with YO of previous row, K1.
Row 2 (WS): K1, *YO, Sl 1, K next st tog with YO of previous row, rep from * to last 2 sts, YO, Sl 1, K1.
Rows 1 and 2 form patt.

Cont straight in patt until back meas 41(42,42,43,43,44)cm/16(16½,16½,17,17,17½)in, ending with a WS row.
Mark each end of last row.

Cont straight in patt until back meas 19(19,20,20,21,21)cm/7½(7½,8,8,8¼,8¼)in from markers, ending with a WS row.

Shape shoulders
Working P1 instead of YO, Sl 1 for patt, cast off 6(7,7,7,8,9) sts at beg of next 4 rows. 57[57,61,65,65,69] sts.

Next row (RS): Working P1 instead of YO, Sl 1 for patt, cast off 7(7,8,8,8,9) sts, patt to end. 50[50,53,57,57,60] sts.
Rep last row 3 times more. 29[29,29,33,33,33] sts.

Slip rem sts onto a stitch holder.

FRONT
Using 4mm (US 6) needles, cast on 81(85,89,93,97,105) sts.

Next row (WS): K1, *YO, Sl 1, K1, rep from * to end.

Row 1 (RS): K1, *K next st tog with YO of previous row, YO, Sl 1, rep from * to last 2 sts, K next st tog with YO of previous row, K1.
Row 2 (WS): K1, *YO, Sl 1, K next st tog with YO of previous row, rep from * to last 2 sts, YO, Sl 1, K1.
Rows 1 and 2 form patt.

Cont straight in patt until front meas 41(42,42,43,43,44)cm/16(16½,16½,17,17,17½)in, ending with a WS row.
Mark each end of last row.

Cont straight in patt until front meas 9(9,10,10,11,11)cm/3½(3½,4,4,4½,4½)in from markers, ending with a WS row.

Shape neck
Next row (RS): Patt 29(31,33,33,35,39), K next st tog with YO from previous row and following st, turn, leaving rem sts on a stitch holder. 30[32,34,34,36,40] sts.

Next row (WS): Patt to end.
Next row: Patt to last 2 sts, P2tog. 29[31,33,33,35,39] sts.
Next row: Patt to end.
Next row: Patt to last 2 sts, K next st tog with YO from previous row and last st. 28[30,32,32,34,38] sts.
Rep last 4 rows once more. 26[28,30,30,32,36] sts.

Cont straight in patt until front matches back to start of shoulder shaping, ending with a WS row.

Shape shoulder
Next row (RS): Working P1 instead of YO, Sl 1 for patt, cast off 6(7,7,7,8,9) sts, patt to end. 20[21,23,23,34,27] sts.

Next row (WS): Working P1 instead of YO, Sl 1 for patt, patt to end.
Rep last 2 rows once more. 14[14,16,16,16,18] sts.

Next row (RS): Working P1 instead of YO, Sl 1 for patt, cast off 7(7,8,8,8,9) sts, patt to end. 7[7,8,8,8,9] sts.
Next Row (WS): Working P1 instead of YO, Sl 1 for patt, patt to end.

Working P1 instead of YO, Sl 1 for patt, cast off rem sts.

With RS facing, slip centre 19(19,19,23,23,23) sts onto a stitch holder, rejoin yarn to rem 31(33,35,35,37,41) sts and K first sts tog with YO from previous row and next st, patt to end. 30[32,34,34,36,40] sts.

Next row (WS): Patt to end.
Next row: P2tog, patt to end. 29[31,33,33,35,39] sts.
Next row: Patt to end.
Next row: K first st tog with YO from previous row and next st, patt to end. 28[30,32,32,34,38] sts.
Rep last 4 rows once more. 26[28,30,30,32,36] sts.

Cont straight in patt until front matches back to start of shoulder shaping, ending with a RS row.

Next row (WS): Working P1 instead of YO, Sl 1 for patt, cast off 6(7,7,7,8,9) sts, patt to end. 20[21,23,23,34,27] sts.
Next row (RS): Working P1 instead of YO, Sl 1 for patt, patt to end.
Rep last 2 rows once more. 14[14,16,16,16,18] sts.

Next row (WS): Working P1 instead of YO, Sl 1 for patt, cast off 7(7,8,8,8,9) sts, patt to end. 7[7,8,8,8,9] sts.
Next row (RS): Working P1 instead of YO, Sl 1 for patt, patt to end.

Working P1 instead of YO, Sl 1 for patt, cast off rem sts.

SLEEVES (make two)
Using 4mm (US 6) needles, cast on 67(67,71,71,75,75) sts.

Next row (WS): K1, *YO, Sl 1, K1, rep from * to end.

Work straight in patt as for back until work meas 20cm/8in, ending with a WS row.

Next row (RS): K first st tog with YO and next st, patt to last 2 sts, k next st tog with YO and last st.
65[65,69,69,73,73] sts.
Cont straight in patt for 7(7,7,9,9,9) rows.

Next row (RS): P2tog, patt to last 2 sts, P2tog.
63[63,67,67,71,71] sts.
Cont straight in patt for 7(7,7,9,9,9) rows.

Rep last 16(16,16,18,18,18) rows once more.
59[59,63,63,67,67] sts.

Cont straight in patt until sleeve meas
42(43,44,45,46,47)cm/16½(17,17½,17¾,18¼,18½)in,
ending with a WS row.

Working P1 instead of YO, Sl 1 for patt, cast off.

MAKING UP
Press as described on the information page.
Join right shoulder seam using mattress stitch.

NECKBAND
With RS facing and using 4mm (US 6) needles,
pick up and knit 17 sts down left front neck,
patt 19(19,19,23,23,23) sts from front neck stitch
holder, pick up and knit 16 sts up right front neck,
29(29,29,33,33,33) sts from back neck stitch holder.
81[81,81,89,89,89] sts.

Next row (WS): K1, patt 28(28,28,32,32,32), *YO, Sl 1,
K1, rep from * 7 times more, patt 19(19,19,23,23,23),
K1, **YO, Sl 1, K1, rep from ** to end.

Work straight in patt as for back for 8 rows.

Working P1 instead of YO, Sl 1 for patt, cast off.

Join left shoulder and neckband seam.
Sew in sleeves between markers on front and
back.
Join side and sleeve seams.

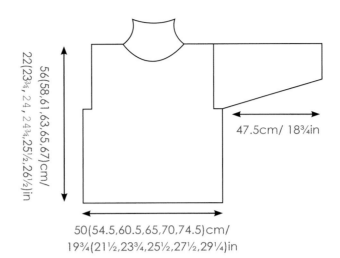

56(58,61,63,65,67)cm/
22(23¾, 24 , 24¾,25½,26½)in

47.5cm/ 18¾in

50(54.5,60.5,65,70,74.5)cm/
19¾(21½,23¾,25½,27½,29¼)in

Bramble

SIZES

To Fit Bust

71 – 76	81 – 86	91 – 97	102 – 107	112 – 117	122 – 127	cm
28 – 30	32 – 34	36 – 38	40 – 42	44 – 46	48 – 50	in

Actual Size

100	109	121	130	140	149	cm
39¼	43	47¾	51¼	55	58¾	in

YARN

Rowan Brushed Fleece

A - 4(4,4,5,5,5) x 50g
(photographed in shade Peat 262)
B - 3(3,3,4,4,4) x 50g
(photographed in shade Crag 253)
C - 1(1,1,2,2,2) x 50g
(photographed in shade Cairn 263)

NEEDLES

5mm (no 6) (US 8) and 6mm (no 4) (US 10) needles

TENSION

13 stitches and 19 rows to 10cm/4in measured
over stocking stitch using 6mm (US 10) needles.

EXTRAS

Stitch holders

BACK

Using 5mm (US 8) needles and yarn A, cast on
65(71,79,85,91,97) sts.
Next row (RS): K1, *P1, K1, rep from * to end.
Next row (WS): P1, *K1, P1, rep from * to end.
Rep last 2 rows of rib until work meas 8cm/3¼in,
ending with a WS row.

Change to 6mm (US 10) needles.

Starting with a K row, work straight in st st until back
meas 12cm/4¾in from cast-on edge, ending with
a WS row.

Change to yarn B.
Cont straight in st st for 32 rows, ending with a
WS row.

Change to yarn A.
Cont straight in st st until back meas
35(36,37,38,39,40)cm/13¾(14¼,14½,15,15½,15¾)in
from cast-on edge, ending with a WS row.

Shape armholes
Cont in st st, cast off 3(3,3,3,4,4) sts at beg of next 2
rows. 59[65,73,79,83,89] sts.

Next row (RS): K2, Sl 1, K1, psso, K to last 4 sts,
K2tog, K2. 57[63,71,77,81,87] sts.
Next row (WS): P2, P2tog, P to last 4 sts, P2togtbl,
P2. 55[61,69,75,79,85] sts.

Next row: K2, Sl 1, K1, psso, K to last 4 sts, K2tog, K2.
53[59,67,73,77,83] sts.
Next row: Purl.
Rep last 2 rows 1(1,2,2,2,2) time(s) more.
51[57,63,69,73,79] sts.

Work 10(10,4,4,0,0) rows straight.

Change to yarn C.
Cont straight in st st until armhole meas
18(19,21,22,23,24)cm/7(7½,8¼,8¾,9,9½)in, ending
with a WS row.

Shape shoulders
Cont in st st, cast off 4(5,6,7,8,9) sts at beg of next 4
rows. 35[37,39,41,41,43] sts.
Cast off 5(6,7,7,7,8) sts at beg of next 2 rows.
25[25,25,27,27,27] sts.

Slip rem sts onto a stitch holder.

FRONT
Using 5mm (US 8) needles and yarn A, cast on
65(71,79,85,91,97) sts.
Work in rib as for back until front meas 8cm/3¼in,
ending with a WS row.

Change to 6mm (US 10) needles.

Starting with a K row, work straight in st st until front
meas 12cm/4¾in from cast-on edge, ending with
a WS row.

Change to yarn B.
Cont straight in st st for 32 rows, ending with a WS
row.

Change to yarn A.
Cont straight in st st until front meas
35(36,37,38,39,40)cm/13¾(14¼,14½,15,15½,15¾)in
from cast-on edge, ending with a WS row.

Shape armholes
Cont in st st, cast off 3(3,3,3,4,4) sts at beg of next 2
rows. 59[65,73,79,83,89] sts.

Next row (RS): K2, Sl 1, K1, psso, K to last 4 sts,
K2tog, K2. 57[63,71,77,81,87] sts.
Next row (WS): P2, P2tog, P to last 4 sts, P2togtbl,
P2. 55[61,69,75,79,85] sts.

Next row: K2, Sl 1, K1, psso, K to last 4 sts, K2tog, K2.
53[59,67,73,77,83] sts.
Next row: Purl.
Rep last 2 rows 1(1,2,2,2,2) time(s) more.
51[57,63,69,73,79] sts.

Work 10(10,4,4,0,0) rows straight.

Change to yarn C.
Cont straight in st st until armhole meas
12(13,14,15,16,17)cm/4¾(5¼,5½,6,6¼,6¾)in,
ending with a WS row.

Shape neck
Next row (RS): K16(19,22,24,26,29), K2tog,
K2, turn, leaving rem sts on a stitch holder.
19[22,25,27,29,32] sts.

Next row (WS): P2, P2tog, P to end.
18[21,24,26,28,31] sts.
Next row (RS): K to last 4 sts, K2tog, K2.
17[20,23,25,27,30] sts.
Rep last 2 rows once more. 15[18,21,23,25,28] sts.

Next row (WS): Purl.
Next row (RS): K to last 4 sts, K2tog, K2.
14[17,20,22,24,27] sts.

Rep last 2 rows once more. 13[16,19,21,23,26] sts.

Cont straight in st st until front meas same as back
to start of shoulder shaping, ending with a WS row.

Shape shoulder
Cont in st st, cast off 4(5,6,7,8,9) sts at beg of next
and foll alt row. 5[6,7,7,7,8] sts.
Next row (WS): Purl.
Cast off.

With RS facing, slip centre 11(11,11,13,13,13)
sts onto a stitch holder, rejoin yarn to rem
20(23,26,28,30,33) sts and K2, Sl 1, K1, psso, K to
end. 19[22,25,27,29,32] sts.

Next row (WS): P to last 4 sts, P2togtbl, P2.
18[21,24,26,28,31] sts.
Next row (RS): K2, Sl 1, K1, psso, K to end.
17[20,23,25,27,30] sts.
Rep last 2 rows once more. 15[18,21,23,25,28] sts.

Next row (WS): Purl.
Next row (RS): K2, Sl 1, K1, psso, K to end.
14[17,20,22,24,27] sts.
Rep last 2 rows once more. 13[16,19,21,23,26] sts.

Cont straight in st st until front matches back to start of shoulder shaping, ending with a RS row.

Shape shoulder
Cont in st st, cast off 4(5,6,7,8,9) sts at beg of next and foll alt row. 5[6,7,7,7,8] sts.
Next row (RS): Knit.
Cast off.

SLEEVES (make two)
Using 5mm (US 8) needles and yarn A, cast on 31(33,33,35,35,37) sts.
Work in rib as for back until sleeve meas 8cm/3¼in, ending with a WS row.

Change to 6mm (US 10) needles.

Starting with a K row, cont straight in st st for 4 rows.

Next row (RS): K2, M1, K to last 2 sts, M1, K2.
33[35,35,37,37,39] sts.
Cont in st st, working inc as set above, inc 1 st at each end of every foll 10th(10th,6th,6th,4th,4th) row to 37(39,41,43,47,47) sts.
Cont straight in st st for 7(5,5,5,1,3) rows, ending with a WS row.

Change to yarn B.
Cont straight in st st for 2(4,2,0,6,4) rows.
Cont in st st, working inc as set above, inc 1 st at each end of next and every foll 10th(10th,8th,6th,8th,6th) row to 43(45,49,53,55,57) sts.
Cont straight in st st for 9(7,5,7,1,5) rows, ending with a WS row.

Change to yarn A.
Cont straight in st st until sleeve meas 47.5cm/18¾in, ending with a WS row.

Shape sleeve top
Cont in st st, cast off 3(3,3,3,4,4) sts at beg of next 2 rows. 37[39,43,47,47,49] sts.

Next row (RS): K2, Sl 1, K1, psso, K to last 4 sts, K2tog, K2. 35[37,41,45,45,47] sts.
Cont in st st, working dec as set above, dec 1 st at each end of foll 4th row 3(3,2,2,1,1) times more. 29[31,37,41,43,45] sts.
Next row (WS): Purl.

Change to yarn C.
Cont straight in st st for 0(0,0,0,2,2) rows.
Next row (RS): K2, Sl 1, K1, psso, K to last 4 sts, K2tog, K2. 27[29,35,39,41,43] sts.
Next row (WS): Purl.
Rep last 2 rows 2(3,6,7,8,8) times more.
23[23,23,25,25,27] sts.

Next row (RS): K2, Sl 1, K1, psso, K to last 4 sts, K2tog, K2. 21[21,21,23,23,25] sts.
Next row (WS): P2, P2tog, P to last 4 sts, P2togtbl, P2. 19[19,19,21,21,23] sts.

Cast off 3 sts at beg of next 2 rows.
13[13,13,15,15,17] sts.

Cast off.

MAKING UP
Press as described on the information page.
Join right shoulder seam using mattress stitch.

NECKBAND
With RS facing, using yarn C and 5mm (US 8) needles, pick up and knit 13(13,15,15,15,15) sts down left front neck, knit 11(11,11,13,13,13) sts from front neck stitch holder, pick up and knit 13(13,15,15,15,15) sts up right front neck, knit 25(25,25,27,27,27) sts from back neck stitch holder increasing 1 st at centre of these sts. 63[63,67,71,71,71] sts.

Next row (WS): P1, *K1, P1, rep from * to end.
Next row (RS): K1, *P1, K1, rep from * to end.
Rep last 2 rows of rib until neckband meas 8cm/3¼in, ending with a WS row.
Cast off loosely in rib.

Join left shoulder and neckband seam.
Sew in sleeves, matching colour blocks.
Join side and sleeve seams.

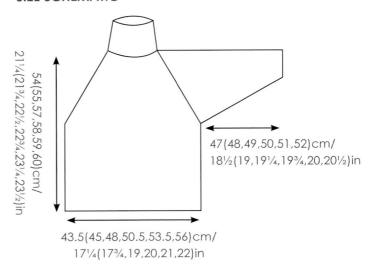

SIZE SCHEMATIC

54(55,57,58,59,60)cm/
21¼(21¾,22½,22¾,23¼,23½)in

47(48,49,50,51,52)cm/
18½(19,19¼,19¾,20,20½)in

43.5(45,48,50.5,53.5,56)cm/
17¼(17¾,19,20,21,22)in

Clover

SIZES

To Fit Bust

71 – 76	81 – 86	91 – 97	102 – 107	112 – 117	122 – 127	cm
28 – 30	32 – 34	36 – 38	40 – 42	44 – 46	48 – 50	in

Actual Size

87	90	96	101	107	112	cm
34¼	35½	37¾	39¾	42¼	44	in

YARN

Rowan Cocoon
7(7,8,8,9,9) x 100g balls of Rowan Cocoon
(pictured in shade Misty Blue 827)

NEEDLES

5mm (no 6) (US 8) and 6mm (no 4) (US 10) needles.

TENSION

14 stitches and 20 rows to 10cm/4in measured
over stocking stitch using 6mm (US 10) needles.

EXTRAS

Stitch holders
Stitch markers

BACK

Using 5mm (US 8) needles, cast on
61(63,67,71,75,79) sts.

Next row (RS): K1, *P1, K1, rep from * to end.
Next row (WS): P1, *K1, P1, rep from * to end.
Rep last 2 rows of rib until back meas 20cm/8in,
ending with a WS row.

Change to 6mm (US 10) needles.

Starting with a K row, cont in st st until back meas
37(37,38,38,38,38)cm/14½(14½,15,15,15,15)in,
ending with a WS row.

Mark each end of last row.

Shape raglan armholes

Cont in st st, cast off 1(1,2,2,3,4) sts at beg of next 2
rows. 59[61,63,67,69,71] sts.

Next row (RS): K2, SI 1, K1, psso, K to last 4 sts, K2tog, K2. 57[59,61,65,67,69] sts.

Next row (WS): Purl.
Rep last 2 rows 15(16,17,18,19,20) times more. 27[27,27,29,29,29] sts.

Slip rem sts onto a stitch holder.

FRONT
Using 5mm (US 8) needles, cast on 61(63,67,71,75,79) sts.

Work in rib as for back until front meas 20cm/8in, ending with a WS row.

Change to 6mm (US 10) needles.

Starting with a K row, cont in st st until front meas 37(37,38,38,38,38)cm/14½(14½,15,15,15,15)in, ending with a WS row.

Mark each end of last row.

Shape raglan armholes
Cont in st st, cast off 1(1,2,2,3,4) sts at beg of next 2 rows. 59[61,63,67,69,71] sts.

Next row (RS): K2, SI 1, K1, psso, K to last 4 sts, K2tog, K2. 57[59,61,65,67,69] sts.
Next row (WS): Purl.
Rep last 2 rows 7(8,9,10,11,12) times more. 43[43,43,45,45,45] sts.

Shape neck
Next row (RS): K2, SI 1, K1, psso, K8, K2tog, K2, turn, leaving rem sts on a stitch holder. 14 sts.

Next row (WS): Purl.
Next row (RS): K2, SI 1, K1, psso, K to last 4 sts, K2tog, K2. 12 sts.
Rep last 2 rows twice more. 8 sts.

Next row (WS): Purl.
Next row (RS): K2, SI 1, K1, psso, K2tog, K2. 6 sts.
Next row: Purl.
Next row: K1, SI 1, K1, psso, K2tog, K1. 4 sts
Next row: Purl.
Next row: K1, SI 1, K2tog, psso. 2 sts.
Next row: Purl.
Next row: SI 1, K1, psso and fasten off.

With RS facing, slip centre 11(11,11,13,13,13) sts onto a stitch holder, rejoin yarn to rem 16 sts and K2, SI 1, K1, psso, K8, K2tog, K2. 14 sts.

Next row (WS): Purl.
Next row (RS): K2, SI 1, K1, psso, K to last 4 sts, K2tog, K2. 12 sts.
Rep last 2 rows twice more. 8 sts.

Next row (WS): Purl.
Next row (RS): K2, SI 1, K1, psso, K2tog, K2. 6 sts.
Next row: Purl.
Next row: K1, SI 1, K1, psso, K2tog, K1. 4 sts.
Next row: Purl.
Next row: K3tog, K1. 2 sts.
Next row: Purl.
Next row: K2tog and fasten off.

SLEEVES (make two)
Using 5mm (US 8) needles, cast on 39(41,43,45,45,47) sts.
Work in rib as for back until sleeve meas 10cm/4in, ending with a WS row.

Change to 6mm (US 10) needles.

Starting with a K row, work 4 rows in st st.

Next row (RS): K2, M1, K to last 2 sts, M1, K2. 41[43,45,47,47,49] sts.

Cont in st st, working inc as set above, inc 1 st at each end of 2(2,3,4,5,5) foll 22nd(22nd,16th,12th,10th,10th) rows. 45[47,51,55,57,59] sts.

Cont straight in st st until sleeve meas 47(48,49,50,51,52)cm/18½(19,19¼,19¾,20,20½)in, ending with a WS row.

Mark each end of last row.

Shape raglan seam
Cont in st st, cast off 1(1,2,2,3,4) sts at beg of next 2 rows. 43[45,47,51,51,51] sts.

Next row (RS): K2, SI 1, K1, psso, K to last 4 sts, K2tog, K2. 41[43,45,49,49,49] sts.
Next row (WS): P2, P2tog, P to last 4 sts, P2togtbl, P2. 39[41,43,47,47,47] sts.
Rep last 2 rows 1(1,1,2,1,0) times more. 35[37,39,39,43,47] sts.

Next row (RS): K2, SI 1, K1, psso, K to last 4 sts, K2tog, K2. 33[35,37,37,41,45] sts.
Next row (WS): Purl.
Rep last 2 rows 12(13,14,14,16,18) times more. 9 sts.

Next row (RS): K2, SI 1, K1, psso, K1, K2tog, K2. 7 sts.
Next row (WS): Purl.
Cast off.

MAKING UP
Press as described on the information page.
Join right back and both front raglan seams using mattress stitch.

NECKBAND
With RS facing and using 5mm (US 8) needles, pick up and knit 6 sts along left sleeve top, 17 sts down left front neck, work across sts from front stitch holder as follows: K2(2,2,3,3,3), *Kfb, K2, rep from * once more, Kfb, K2(2,2,3,3,3), then pick up and knit 17 sts up right front neck, 5 sts from right sleeve top, work across sts from back stitch holder as follows: K1(1,1,2,2,2), *Kfb, K3, rep from * 5 times more, Kfb, K1(1,1,2,2,2). 93[93,93,97,97,97] sts.

Working in rib as for back, work in rib for 20cm/8in, ending with a WS row.
Cast off loosely in rib.

Join remaining raglan and neckband seams, reversing seam on neckband 5cm/2in up from neck edge.
Join side and sleeve seams.

SIZE SCHEMATIC

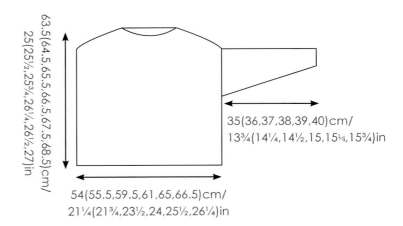

63.5(64.5,65.5,66.5,67.5,68.5)cm/
25(25½,25¾,26¼,26½,27)in

35(36,37,38,39,40)cm/
13¾(14¼,14½,15,15¼,15¾)in

54(55.5,59.5,61,65,66.5)cm/
21¼(21¾,23½,24,25½,26¼)in

Maize

SIZES

To Fit Bust

71 – 76	81 – 86	91 – 97	102 – 107	112 – 117	122 – 127	cm
28 – 30	32 – 34	36 – 38	40 – 42	44 – 46	48 – 50	in

Actual Size

108	111	119	122	130	133	cm
42½	43¾	46¾	48	51¼	52¼	in

YARN

Rowan Cashmere Tweed
22(23,24,25,26,27) x 25g balls of Rowan Cashmere
Tweed (photographed in Oats 001)

NEEDLES

4mm (no 8) (US 6) needles

TENSION

35 stitches and 38 rows to 10cm/4in measured
over patt using 4mm (US 6) needles.

EXTRAS

Cable needle
Stitch holders

SPECIAL ABBREVIATIONS

C4F – slip next 2 sts onto cable needle and hold at
front of work, K2, then K2 sts from cable needle.
C4B – slip next 2 sts onto cable needle and hold at
back of work, K2, then K2 sts from cable needle.

CABLE PATTERN

Row 1 (WS): P16.
Row 2 (RS): K4, C4B, C4F, K4.
Row 3: As row 1.
Row 4: K2, C4B, K4, C4F, K2.
Row 5: As row 1.
Row 6: C4B, K8, C4F.

BACK

Using 4mm needles (US 6), cast on
189(195,208,214,227,233) sts.

Next row (WS): K0(2,0,2,0,2), P0(1,0,1,0,1), K1, *work
row 1 of cable pattern, K1, P1, K1, rep from * to last
17(20,17,20,17,20) sts, work row 1 of cable pattern,
K1, P0(1,0,1,0,1), K0(2,0,2,0,2).
Next row (RS): P0(2,0,2,0,2), K0(1,0,1,0,1), P1, *work
row 2 of cable pattern, P1, K1, P1, rep from * to
last 17(20,17,20,17,20) sts, *work row 2 of cable
pattern, P1, K0(1,0,1,0,1), P0(2,0,2,0,2).
Working rows as set above, starting with row

3 of cable pattern and working cable rows 1-6 throughout, cont in patt until back meas 40(40,41,41,41,41)cm/15¾(15¾,16¼,16¼,16¼,16¼) in, ending with a WS row.

Mark each end of last row.

Cont in patt until back meas 21(22,22,23,24,25) cm/8¼(8¾,8¾,9,9½,10)in from markers, ending with a WS row.

Shape shoulders
Cont in patt, cast off 10(11,12,12,13,14) sts at beg of next 8(8,8,6,8,8) rows. 109[107,112,142,123,121] sts.
Cont in patt, cast off 11(10,11,13,14,13) sts at beg of next 2(2,2,4,2,2) rows. 87[87,90,90,95,95] sts.

Slip rem sts onto a stitch holder.

FRONT
Using 4mm needles (US 6), cast on 189(195,208,214,227,233) sts.

Next row (WS): K0(2,0,2,0,2), P0(1,0,1,0,1), K1, *work row 1 of cable pattern, K1, P1, K1, rep from * to last 17(20,17,20,17,20) sts, work row 1 of cable pattern, K1, P0(1,0,1,0,1), K0(2,0,2,0,2).
Next row (RS): P0(2,0,2,0,2), K0(1,0,1,0,1), P1, *work row 2 of cable pattern, P1, K1, P1, rep from * to last 17(20,17,20,17,20) sts, *work row 2 of cable pattern, P1, K0(1,0,1,0,1), P0(2,0,2,0,2).
Working rows as set above, starting with row 3 of cable pattern and working cable rows 1-6 throughout, cont in patt until front meas 40(40,41,41,41,41)cm/15¾(15¾,16¼,16¼,16¼,16¼) in, ending with a WS row.

Mark each end of last row.

Cont in patt until front meas 20.5(21.5,21.5,22.5,23.5,24.5) cm/8(8½,8½,8¾,9¼,9½)in from markers, ending with a WS row.

Shape neck
Keep cable pattern correct throughout.
Next row (RS): Patt 58(61,66,69,73,76) sts, turn, leaving rem sts on a stitch holder.
Next row (WS): P2tog, patt to end. 57[60,65,68,72,75] sts

Shape shoulder
Next row (RS): Cast off 10(11,12,12,13,14), patt to last 2 sts, K2tog. 46[48,52,55,58,60] sts.

Next row (WS): P2tog, patt to end. 45[47,51,54,57,59] sts.
Rep last 2 rows twice more. 21[21,23,26,27,27] sts

Next row (RS): Cast off 10(11,12,13,13,14), patt to end. 11[10,11,13,14,13] sts.
Next row (WS): Patt to end.

Cast off.

With RS facing, slip centre 73(73,76,76,81,81) sts onto a stitch holder, rejoin yarn to rem 58(61,66,69,73,76) sts and patt to end.
Next row (WS): Patt to last 2 sts, P2tog. 57[60,65,68,72,75] sts.

Next row (RS): K2tog, patt to end. 56[59,64,67,71,74] sts.
Next row (WS): Cast off 10(11,12,12,13,14), patt to last 2 sts, P2tog. 45[47,51,54,57,59] sts.
Rep last 2 rows twice more. 21[21,23,26,27,27] sts.

Next row (RS): Patt to end
Next row (WS): Cast off 10(11,12,13,13,14), patt to end. 11[10,11,13,14,13] sts.
Next row: Patt to end.

Cast off.

SLEEVES (make two)
Using 4mm (US 6) needles, cast on 87(91,98,98,102,104) sts.
Next row (WS): P4(6,0,0,2,3), K1, P1, K1, *work row 1 of cable pattern, K1, P1, K1, rep from * to last 4(6,0,0,2,3) sts, P4(6,0,0,2,3).
Next row (RS): K4(6,0,0,2,3), P1, K1, P1, *work row 2 of cable pattern, P1, K1, P1, rep from * to last 4(6,0,0,2,3) sts, K4(6,0,0,2,3).
Working rows as set above, starting with row 3 of cable pattern and working cable rows 1-6 throughout, cont in patt for 4 rows, ending with a RS row.

Next row (WS): Kfb, patt to last st, Kfb. 89[93,100,100,104,106] sts.

Cont in patt, working inc as set above, inc 1 st at each end of 29(30,27,30,32,34) foll 4th rows, incorporating increased sts into st st. 147[153,154,160,168,174] sts.

Cont straight in patt for a few rows until sleeve meas 35(36,37,38,39,40) cm/13¾(14¼,14½,15,15½,15¾)in, ending with a WS row.

Working K2tog twice instead of C4B or C4F for cable pattern, cast off in patt.

MAKING UP
Press as described on the information page.
Join right shoulder seam using mattress stitch.

NECKBAND
With RS facing and using 4mm (US 6) needles, pick up and knit 9 sts down left front neck, work across sts from front neck stitch holder as follows: K1(1,1,1,5,5), [K2tog, K2] 3 (3,1,1,3,3) times, K2tog, *K5, [K2tog, K2] 3 times, K2tog, rep from * 1(1,2,2,1,1) times more, K5, [K2tog, K2] 3 (3,1,1,3,3) times, K2tog, K1(1,1,1,5,5), pick up and knit 9 sts up right front neck, work across sts from back neck stitch holder as follows: K1(1,4,4,1,1), [K2tog, K2] 0(0,2,2,1,1) times, K2tog, **K5, [K2tog, K2] 3 times, K2tog, rep from ** 3(3,2,2,3,3) times more, K5, [K2tog, K2] 0(0,2,2,1,1) times, K2tog, K1(1,4,4,1,1). 144[144,150,150,158,158] sts.

Cast off.

Join left shoulder and neckband seams.
Sew cast-off edge of sleeves between markers on back and front.
Join side and sleeve seams.

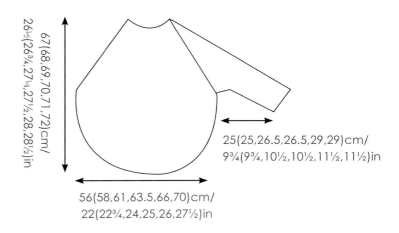

67(68,69,70,71,72)cm/
26½(26¾,27¼,27½,28,28½)in

25(25,26.5,26.5,29,29)cm/
9¾(9¾,10½,10½,11½,11½)in

56(58,61,63.5,66,70)cm/
22(22¾,24,25,26,27½)in

Amber

SIZES
To Fit Bust

71 – 76	81 – 86	91 – 97	102 – 107	112 – 117	122 – 127	cm
28 – 30	32 – 34	36 – 38	40 – 42	44 – 46	48 – 50	in

Actual Size

112	116	122	127	132	140	cm
44	45¾	48	50	52	55	in

YARN
Rowan Felted Tweed
7(7,8,8,9,9) x 50g balls of Rowan Felted Tweed
(photographed in shade Alabaster 197)

NEEDLES
3.75mm (no 9) (US 5) needles

TENSION
22 stitches and 30 rows to 10cm/4in measured
over stocking stitch using 3.75mm (US 5) needles.

EXTRAS
Stitch holders
4 blue stitch markers
8 red stitch markers
8 green stitch markers

BACK
Using 3.75mm (US 5) needles, cast on 34 sts.
Starting with a P row, work 1 row in st st, ending
with a WS row.

Shape hem edge
Cont in st st, cast on 5(5,5,5,6,6) sts at beg of next 6
rows. 64[64,64,64,70,70] sts.
Cast on 3(3,4,4,4,5) sts at beg of next 4(6,6,8,8,8)
rows. 76[82,88,96,102,110] sts.
Cast on 2 sts at beg of next 10 rows.
96[102,108,116,122,130] sts.
Place blue marker at each end of last row.

Next row (RS): K2, M1, K to last 2 sts, M1, K2.
98[104,110,118,124,132] sts.
Next row (WS): Purl.
Rep last 2 rows 8(7,7,6,6,6) times more.
114[118,124,130,136,144) sts.

Cont in st st, working inc as set above, inc 1 st at

each end of next and 2 foll 4th rows, then on 2 foll 6th rows. 124[128,134,140,146,154] sts.

Cont straight in st st until back measures 24cm/9½in from cast-on edge, ending with a WS row.
Place red marker at each end of last row.

Shape raglan armhole
Next row (RS): K2, Sl 1, K1, psso, K to last 4 sts, K2tog, K2. 122[126,132,138,144,152] sts.
Cont in st st, working dec as set above, dec 1 st at each end of 16(17,15,15,14,11) foll 4th rows. 90[92,102,108,116,130] sts.
Cont in st st, working dec as set above, dec 1 st at each end of 19(19,24,25,29,36) foll alt rows. 52[54,54,58,58,58] sts.
Next row (WS): Purl.

Shape neck
Next row (RS): K2, Sl 1, K1, psso, K8(8,8,11,11,11), K2tog, K2, turn, leaving rem sts on a stitch holder. 14[14,14,17,17,17] sts.

Next row (WS): P2, P2tog, P to end. 13[13,13,16,16,16] sts.
Next row (RS): K2, Sl 1, K1, psso, K to last 4 sts, K2tog, K2. 11[11,11,14,14,14] sts.
Rep last 2 rows 1(1,1,2,2,2) times more. 8 sts.

Next row (WS): P2, P2tog, P to end. 7 sts.
Next row (RS): K2, Sl 1, K2tog, psso, K2. 5 sts.
Next row: Purl.
Next row: K1, Sl 1, K2tog, psso, K1. 3 sts.
Next row: Purl.
Next row: K1, Sl 1, K1, psso. 2 sts.
Next row: Purl.
Next row: Sl 1, K1, psso and fasten off.

With RS facing, slip centre 20(22,22,20,20,20) sts onto a stitch holder, rejoin yarn to rem 16(16,16,19,19,19) sts and K2, Sl1, K1, psso, K to last 4 sts, K2tog, K2. 14[14,14,17,17,17] sts.

Next row (WS): P to last 4 sts, P2togtbl, P2. 13[13,13,16,16,16] sts.
Next row (RS): K2, Sl 1, K1, psso, K to last 4 sts, K2tog, K2. 11[11,11,14,14,14] sts.
Rep last 2 rows 1(1,1,2,2,2) times more. 8 sts.

Next row (WS): P to last 4 sts, P2togtbl, P2. 7 sts.
Next row (RS): K2, Sl 1, K2tog, psso, K2. 5 sts.
Next row: Purl.
Next row: K1, Sl 1, K2tog, psso, K1. 3 sts.
Next row: Purl.

Next row: K2tog, K1. 2 sts.
Next row: Purl.
Next row: K2tog and fasten off.

FRONT
Using 3.75mm (US 5) needles, cast on 34 sts.
Starting with a P row, work 1 row in st st, ending with a WS row.

Shape hem edge
Cont in st st, cast on 5(5,5,5,6,6) sts at beg of next 6 rows. 64[64,64,64,70,70] sts.
Cast on 3(3,4,4,4,5) sts at beg of next 4(6,6,8,8,8) rows. 76[82,88,96,102,110] sts.
Cast on 2 sts at beg of next 10 rows. 96[102,108,116,122,130] sts.
Place blue marker at each end of last row.

Next row (RS): K2, M1, K to last 2 sts, M1, K2. 98[104,110,118,124,132] sts.
Next row (WS): Purl.
Rep last 2 rows 8(7,7,6,6,6) times more. 114[118,124,130,136,144] sts.

Cont in st st, working inc as set above, inc 1 st at each end of next and 2 foll 4th rows, then on 2 foll 6th rows. 124[128,134,140,146,154] sts.

Cont straight in st st until front measures 24cm/9½in from cast-on edge, ending with a WS row.
Place red marker at each end of last row.

Shape raglan armhole
Next row (RS): K2, Sl 1, K1, psso, K to last 4 sts, K2tog, K2. 122[126,132,138,144,152] sts.
Cont in st st, working dec as set above, dec 1 st at each end of 16(17,15,15,14,11) foll 4th rows. 90[92,102,108,116,130] sts.
Cont in st st, working dec as above, dec 1 st at each end of 13(13,18,18,22,29) foll alt rows. 64[66,66,72,72,72] sts.
Next row (WS): Purl.

Shape neck
Next row (RS): K2, Sl 1, K1, psso, K19(19,19,23,23,23), K2tog, K2, turn, leaving rem sts on a stitch holder. 25[25,25,29,29,29] sts.

Next row (WS): P2, P2tog, P to end. 24[24,24,28,28,28] sts.
Next row (RS): K2, Sl 1, K1, psso, K to last 4 sts, K2tog, K2. 22[22,22,26,26,26] sts.
Rep last 2 rows once more. 19[19,19,23,23,23] sts.

Next row (WS): Purl.
Next row (RS): K2, Sl 1, K1, psso, K to last 4 sts, K2tog, K2. 17[17,17,21,21,21] sts.
Rep last 2 rows 5(5,5,7,7,7) times more. 7 sts.

Next row (WS): Purl.
Next row (RS): K2, Sl 1, K2tog, psso, K2. 5 sts.
Next row: Purl.
Next row: K1, Sl 1, K2tog, psso, K1. 3 sts.
Next row: Purl.
Next row: K1, Sl 1, K1, psso. 2 sts.
Next row: Purl.
Next row: Sl 1, K1, psso and fasten off.

With RS facing, slip centre 10(12,12,10,10,10) sts onto a stitch holder, rejoin yarn to rem 27(27,27,31,31,31) sts and K2, Sl 1, K1, psso, K to last 4 sts, K2tog, K2. 25[25,25,29,29,29] sts.

Next row (WS): P to last 4 sts, P2togtbl, P2. 24[24,24,28,28,28] sts.
Next row (RS): K2, Sl 1, K1, psso, K to last 4 sts, K2tog, K2. 22[22,22,26,26,26] sts.
Rep last 2 rows once more. 19[19,19,23,23,23] sts.

Next row (WS): Purl.
Next row (RS): K2, Sl 1, K1, psso, K to last 4 sts, K2tog, K2. 17[17,17,21,21,21] sts.
Rep last 2 rows 5(5,5,7,7,7) times more. 7 sts.

Next row (WS): Purl.
Next row (RS): K2, Sl 1, K2tog, psso, K2. 5 sts.
Next row: Purl.
Next row: K1, Sl 1, K2tog, psso, K1. 3 sts.
Next row: Purl.
Next row: K2tog, K1. 2 sts.
Next row: Purl.
Next row: K2tog and fasten off.

SLEEVES (make two)
Using 3.75mm (US 5) needles, cast on 41(43,45,47,49,51) sts.
Next row (RS): K1, *P1, K1, rep from * to end.
Next row (WS): P1, *K1, P1, rep from * to end.
Rep last 2 rows of rib until sleeve meas 6cm/2½in, ending with a WS row.

Next row (RS): K2, M1, K to last 2 sts, M1, K2. 43[45,47,49,51,53]sts.
Cont in st st, working inc as set above, inc 1 st at each end of 8(8,6,6,2,2) foll alt rows, then on 9(9,11,11,15,15) foll 4th rows. 79[81,83,85,87,89] sts.
Cont straight in st st for 3 rows, ending after a WS row.

Place green marker at each end of last row.

Cont straight in st st for 6 rows, ending after a WS row.
Place red marker at each end of last row.

Shape raglan top

Next row (RS): K2, Sl 1, K1, psso, K to last 4 sts, K2tog, K2. 77[79,81,83,85,87] sts.
Cont in st st, working dec as set above, dec 1 st at each end of 21(22,22,23,24,24) foll 4th rows. 35[35,37,37,37,39] sts.

Cont in st st, working dec as set above, dec at each end of 14(14,15,15,15,16) foll alt rows. 7 sts.

Next row (WS): Purl.
Next row (RS): K2, Sl 1, K2tog, psso, K2. 5 sts.
Next row: Purl.
Cast off.

MAKING UP

HEM EDGING
With RS facing, using 3.75mm (US 5) needles and starting at red marker, pick up and knit 45(44,44,43,43,43) sts between red and blue marker along lower edge of back, 99(105,111,119,125,133) sts between blue markers and 45(44,44,43,43,43) sts between blue and red marker. 189[193,199,205,211,219] sts.

Next row (WS): P1, *K1, P1, rep from * to end.
Next row (RS): K1, *P1, K1, rep from * to end.
Rep last 2 rows of rib until edging meas 2cm/¾in.
Place green marker at each end of last row.
Cont in rib until work meas 2cm/¾in from green marker, ending with a WS row.
Cast off loosely in rib.

Work front hem edging as back hem edging.

Press as described on the information page.
Lap top edges of back hem edging over top edges of front hem edging and secure in position. Matching colour markers, join right back and both front raglan seams using mattress stitch.

NECKBAND

With RS facing and using 3.75mm (US 5) needles, pick up and knit 4 sts along left sleeve top, 24(24,24,28,28,28) sts down left front neck, knit

10(12,12,10,10,10) sts from front neck stitch holder, pick up and knit 24(24,24,28,28,28) sts up right front neck, 3 sts from right sleeve top, 12(12,12,14,14,14) sts down right back neck, knit 20(22,22,20,20,20) sts from back neck stitch holder, pick up and knit 12(12,12,14,14,14) sts up left back neck. 109[113,113,121,121,121] sts.

Next row (WS): P1, *K1, P1, rep from * to end.
Next row (RS): K1, *P1, K1, rep from * to end.
Rep last 2 rows of rib until neckband meas 4cm/1½in, ending with a WS row.
Cast off loosely in rib.

Join rem raglan and neckband seams. Join side and sleeve seams.

information

sizing guide

To help you enjoy a great knitting experience and a well fitting garment please refer to our sizing guide which conforms to standard clothing sizes. Dimensions in our sizing guide are body measurements, not garment dimensions, please refer to the size diagram for this measurment.

SIZING GUIDE

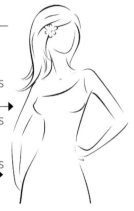

UK SIZE	XS	S	M	L	XL	XXL	
DUAL SIZE	4/6	8/10	12/14	16/18	20/22	24/26	
To fit bust	28 – 30	32 – 34	36 – 38	40 – 42	44 – 46	48 – 50	inches
	71 – 76	81 – 86	91 - 97	102 – 107	112 – 117	122 – 127	cm
To fit waist	20 – 22	24 – 26	28 – 30	32 – 34	36 – 38	40 – 42	inches
	51 – 56	61 – 66	71 – 76	81 – 86	91 – 97	102 – 107	cm
To fit hips	30 – 32	34 – 36	38 – 40	42 – 44	46 – 48	50 – 52	inches

SIZING & SIZE DIAGRAM NOTE

The instructions are given for the smallest size. Where they vary, work the figures in brackets for the larger sizes. One set of figures refers to all sizes. Included with most patterns in this magazine is a 'size diagram' - see image on the right, of the finished garment and its dimensions. The measurement shown at the bottom of each 'size diagram' shows the garment width 2.5cm below the armhole shaping. To help you choose the size of garment to knit please refer to the sizing guide. Generally in the majority of designs the welt width (at the cast on edge of the garment) is the same width as the chest. However, some designs are 'A-Line' in shape or flared edge and in these cases welt width will be wider than the chest width.

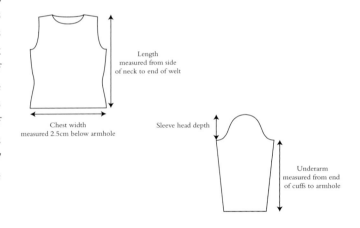

MEASURING GUIDE

For maximum comfort and to ensure the correct fit when choosing a size to knit, please follow the tips below when checking your size. Measure yourself close to your body, over your underwear and don't pull the tape measure too tight!

Bust/chest – measure around the fullest part of the bust/chest and across the shoulder blades.

Waist – measure around the natural waistline, just above the hip bone.

Hips – measure around the fullest part of the bottom.

If you don't wish to measure yourself, note the size of a favourite jumper that you like the fit of. Our sizes are now comparable to the clothing sizes from the major high street retailers, so if your favourite jumper is a size Medium or size 12, then our Medium should be approximately the same fit.

To be extra sure, measure your favourite jumper and then compare these measurements with the Rowan size diagram given at the end of the individual instructions.

Finally, once you have decided which size is best for you, please ensure that you achieve the tension required for the design you wish to knit.

Remember if your tension is too loose, your garment will be bigger than the pattern size and you may use more yarn. If your tension is too tight, your garment could be smaller than the pattern size and you will have yarn left over.

Furthermore if your tension is incorrect, the handle of your fabric will be too stiff or floppy and will not fit properly. It really does make sense to check your tension before starting every project.

information

TENSION

Obtaining the correct tension is perhaps the single factor which can make the difference between a successful garment and a disastrous one. It controls both the shape and size of an article, so any variation, however slight, can distort the finished garment. Different designers feature in our books and it is their tension, given at the start of each pattern, which you must match. We recommend that you knit a square in pattern and/or stocking stitch (depending on the pattern instructions) of perhaps 5 - 10 more stitches and 5 - 10 more rows than those given in the tension note. Mark out the central 10cm square with pins. If you have too many stitches to 10cm try again using thicker needles, if you have too few stitches to 10cm try again using finer needles. Once you have achieved the correct tension your garment will be knitted to the measurements indicated in the
size diagram shown at the end of the pattern.

FINISHING INSTRUCTIONS

After working for hours knitting a garment, it seems a great pity that many garments are spoiled because such little care is taken in the pressing and finishing process. Follow the text below for a truly professional-looking garment.

PRESSING

Block out each piece of knitting and following the instructions on the ball band press the garment pieces, omitting the ribs. Tip: Take special care to press the edges, as this will make sewing up both easier and neater. If the ball band indicates that the fabric is not to be pressed, then covering the blocked out fabric with a damp white cotton cloth and leaving it to stand will have the desired effect. Darn in all ends neatly along the selvage edge or a colour join, as appropriate.

STITCHING

When stitching the pieces together, remember to match areas of colour and texture very carefully where they meet. Use a seam stitch such as back stitch or mattress stitch for all main knitting seams and join all ribs and neckband with mattress stitch, unless otherwise stated.

CONSTRUCTION

Having completed the pattern instructions, join left shoulder and neckband seams as detailed above. Sew the top of the sleeve to the body of the garment using the method detailed in the pattern, referring to the appropriate guide:

Straight cast-off sleeves: Place centre of cast-off edge of sleeve to shoulder seam. Sew top of sleeve to body, using markers as guidelines where applicable.

Square set-in sleeves: Place centre of cast-off edge of sleeve to shoulder seam. Set sleeve head into armhole, the straight sides at top of sleeve to form a neat right-angle to cast-off sts at armhole on back and front.

Shallow set-in sleeves: Place centre of cast off edge of sleeve to shoulder seam. Match decreases at beg of armhole shaping to decreases at top of sleeve. Sew sleeve head into armhole, easing in shapings.

Set-in sleeves: Place centre of cast-off edge of sleeve to shoulder seam. Set in sleeve, easing sleeve head into armhole.

Join side and sleeve seams.
Slip stitch pocket edgings and linings into place.
Sew on buttons to correspond with buttonholes.
Ribbed welts and neckbands and any areas of garter stitch should not be pressed.

PHOTOGRAPHY MODEL INFORMATION

The model in the photography wears a UK dress size 8 and is 5' 8" tall.

The photography garments were knitted in the following sizes; All garments were knitted in a bust size 32-34inches

information

ABBREVIATIONS

alt	alternate
beg	begin(ning)
cm	centimetres
cont	continue
dec	decrease(s)(ing)
DK	double knitting
foll(s)	follow(s)(ing)
g	grams
g st	garter stitch
in	inch(es)
inc	increase(s)(ing)
K	knit
Kfb	knit in front and back of stitch (makes 1 stitch)
M1	make 1 stitch by picking up loop betwee last and next stitch and working into the back of this loop
meas	measures
mm	millimetres
P	purl
patt	pattern
psso	pass slipped stitch over
rem	remain(ing)
rep	repeat
RS	right side of work
Sl 1	slip 1 stitch
st st	stocking stitch
st(s)	stitch(es)
tog	together
WS	wrong side of work

WASHCARE SYMBOLS

machine wash

hand wash

dry clean

iron

do not bleach

drying

Stockists

AUSTRALIA: Australian Country Spinners, Pty Ltd, Level 7, 409 St. Kilda Road, Melbourne Vic 3004.
Tel: 03 9380 3888 Fax: 03 9820 0989 Email: customerservice@auspinners.com.au

AUSTRIA: MEZ Harlander GmbH, Schulhof 6, 1. Stock, 1010 Wien, Austria
Tel: + 00800 26 27 28 00 Fax: (00) 49 7644 802-133
Email: verkauf.harlander@mezcrafts.com

BELGIUM: MEZ crafts Belgium NV, c/o MEZ GmbH, Kaiserstr.1, 79341 Kenzingen Germany
Tel: 0032 (0) 800 77 89 2 Fax: 00 49 7644 802 133 Email: sales.be-nl@mezcrafts.com

BULGARIA: MEZ Crafts Bulgaria EOOD, 7 Magnaurska Shkola Str., BG-1784 Sofia, Bulgaria
Tel: (+359 2) 976 77 41 Fax: (+359 2) 976 77 20 Email: office.bg@mezcrafts.com

CANADA: Sirdar USA Inc. 406 20th Street SE, Hickory, North Carolina, USA 28602
Tel: 828 404 3705 Fax: 828 404 3707 Email: sirdarusa@sirdar.co.uk

CHINA: Commercial agent Mr Victor Li, c/o MEZ GmbH Germany, Kaiserstr. 1, 79341 Kenzingen / Germany
Tel: (86- 21) 13816681825 Email: victor.li@mezcrafts.com

CHINA: SHANGHAI YUJUN CO.,LTD., Room 701 Wangjiao Plaza, No.175 Yan'an (E), 200002 Shanghai, China
Tel: +86 2163739785 Email: jessechang@vip.163.com

CYPRUS: MEZ Crafts Bulgaria EOOD, 7 Magnaurska Shkola Str., BG-1784 Sofia, Bulgaria
Tel: (+359 2) 976 77 41 Fax: (+359 2) 976 77 20
Email: marketing.cy@mezcrafts.com

CZECH REPUBLIC: Coats Czecho s.r.o.Staré Mesto 246 569 32
Tel: (420) 461616633 Email: galanterie@coats.com

DENMARK: Carl J. Permin A/S Egegaardsvej 28 DK-2610 Rødovre
Tel: (45) 36 72 12 00 Email: permin@permin.dk

ESTONIA: MEZ Crafts Estonia OÜ, Ampri tee 9/4, 74001 Viimsi Harjumaa
Tel: +372 630 6252 Email: info.ee@mezcrafts.com

FINLAND: Prym Consumer Finland Oy, Huhtimontie 6, 04200 KERAVA
Tel: +358 9 274871

FRANCE: 3bcom, 35 avenue de Larrieu, 31094 Toulouse cedex 01, France
Tel: 0033 (0) 562 202 096 Email: Commercial@3b-com.com

GERMANY: MEZ GmbH, Kaiserstr. 1, 79341 Kenzingen, Germany
Tel: 0049 7644 802 222 Email: kenzingen.vertrieb@mezcrafts.com
Fax: 0049 7644 802 300

GREECE: MEZ Crafts Bulgaria EOOD, 7 Magnaurska Shkola Str., BG-1784 Sofia, Bulgaria
Tel: (+359 2) 976 77 41 Fax: (+359 2) 976 77 20
Email: marketing.gr@mezcrafts.com

HOLLAND: G. Brouwer & Zn B.V., Oudhuijzerweg 69, 3648 AB Wilnis, Netherlands
Tel: 0031 (0) 297-281 557 Email: info@gbrouwer.nl

HONG KONG: East Unity Company Ltd, Unit B2, 7/F., Block B, Kailey Industrial Centre, 12 Fung Yip Street, Chai Wan
Tel: (852)2869 7110 Email: eastunityco@yahoo.com.hk

ICELAND: Carl J. Permin A/S Egegaardsvej 28 DK-2610 Rødovre
Tel: (45) 36 72 12 00 Email: permin@permin.dk

ITALY: Mez Cucirini Italy Srl, Viale Sarca, 223, 20126 MILANO
Tel: 0039 0264109080 Email: servizio.clienti@mezcrafts.com Fax: 02 64109080

JAPAN: Hobbyra Hobbyre Corporation, 23-37, 5-Chome, Higashi-Ohi, Shinagawa-Ku, 140001l Tokyo. Tel: +81334721104
Daidoh International, 3-8-11 Kudanminami Chiyodaku, Hiei Kudan Bldg 5F, 1018619 Tokyo. Tel +81-3-3222-7076, Fax +81-3-3222-7066

KOREA: My Knit Studio, 3F, 144 Gwanhun-Dong, 110-300 Jongno-Gu, Seoul
Tel: 82-2-722-0006 Email: myknit@myknit.com

LATVIA: Coats Latvija SIA, Mukusalas str. 41 b, Riga LV-1004
Tel: +371 67 625173 Fax: +371 67 892758 Email: info.latvia@coats.com

LEBANON: y.knot, Saifi Village, Mkhalissiya Street 162, Beirut
Tel: (961) 1 992211 Fax: (961) 1 315553 Email: y.knot@cyberia.net.lb

LITHUANIA: MEZ Crafts Lithuania UAB, A. Juozapaviciaus str. 6/2, LT-09310 Vilnius
Tel: +370 527 30971 Fax: +370 527 2305 Email: info.lt@mezcrafts.com

LUXEMBOURG: Coats N.V., c/o Coats GmbH, Kaiserstr.1, 79341 Kenzingen, Germany
Tel: 00 49 7644 802 222 Fax: 00 49 7644 802 133
Email: sales.coatsninove@coats.com

MEXICO: Estambres Crochet SA de CV, Aaron Saenz 1891-7Pte, 64650 MONTERREY
TEL +52 (81) 8335-3870 Email: abremer@redmundial.com.mx

NEW ZEALAND: ACS New Zealand, P.O. Box 76199, Northwood, Christchurch, New Zealand
Tel: 64 3 323 6665 Fax: 64 3 323 6660 Email: lynn@impactmg.co.nz

NORWAY: Carl J. Permin A/S Egegaardsvej 28 DK-2610 Rødovre
Tel: (45) 36 72 12 00 E-mail: permin@permin.dk

PORTUGAL: Mez Crafts Portugal, Lda – Av. Vasco da Gama, 774 - 4431-059 V.N, Gaia, Portugal Tel: 00 351 223 770700 Email: sales.iberia@mezcrafts.com

RUSSIA: Family Hobby, 124683, Moskau, Zelenograd, Haus 1505, Raum III
Tel.: 007 (499) 270-32-47 Handtel. 007 916 213 74 04 Email: tv@fhobby.ru
Web: www.family-hobby.ru

SINGAPORE: Golden Dragon Store, BLK 203 Henderson Rd #07-02, 159546 Henderson Indurstrial Park Singapore
Tel: (65) 62753517 Fax: (65) 62767112 Email: gdscraft@hotmail.com

SLOVAKIA: MEZ Crafts Slovakia, s.r.o. Seberíniho 1, 821 03 Bratislava, Slovakia
Tel: +421 2 32 30 31 19 Email: galanteria@mezcrafts.com

SOUTH AFRICA: Arthur Bales LTD, 62 4th Avenue, Linden 2195
Tel: (27) 11 888 2401 Fax: (27) 11 782 6137 Email: arthurb@new.co.za

SPAIN: MEZ Fabra Spain S.A, Avda Meridiana 350, pta 13 D, 08027 Barcelona
Tel: +34 932908400 Fax: +34 932908409 Email: atencion.clientes@mezcrafts.com

SWEDEN: Carl J. Permin A/S Egegaardsvej 28 DK-2610 Rødovre
Tel: (45) 36 72 12 00 E-mail: permin@permin.dk

SWITZERLAND: MEZ Crafts Switzerland GmbH, Stroppelstrasse20, 5417 Untersiggenthal, Switzerland
Tel: +41 00800 2627 2800 Fax: 0049 7644 802 133
Email: verkauf.ch@mezcrafts.com

TURKEY: MEZ Crafts Tekstil A.S, Kavacık Mahallesi, Ekinciler Cad. Necip Fazıl Sok. No.8 Kat: 5, 34810 Beykoz / Istanbul
Tel: +90 216 425 88 10

TAIWAN: Cactus Quality Co Ltd, 7FL-2, No. 140, Sec.2 Roosevelt Rd, Taipei, 10084 Taiwan, R.O.C.
Tel: 00886-2-23656527 Fax: 886-2-23656503 Email: cqcl@ms17.hinet.net

THAILAND: Global Wide Trading, 10 Lad Prao Soi 88, Bangkok 10310
Tel: 00 662 933 9019 Fax: 00 662 933 9110 Email: global.wide@yahoo.com

U.S.A.: Sirdar USA Inc. 406 20th Street SE, Hickory, North Carolina, USA 28602
Tel: 828 404 3705 Fax: 828 404 3707 Email: sirdarusa@sirdar.co.uk

U.K: Mez Crafts U.K, 17F Brooke's Mill, Armitage Bridge, Huddersfield, HD4 7NR
Web: www.mezcrafts.com Tel: 01484 950630

For a more stockists in all countries please logon to www.knitrowan.com

With thanks

Quail Studio would like to thank our superb team of knitters, who work all hours to turn projects around. A big thanks to Jarek and his team for making the photography look fantastic, Our wonderful model Amy Neville for making the garments look amazing, and finally Kandy for technically checking the patterns.

We would also like to thank everyone who buys and knits from our publications. We are constantly evolving our design studio to ensure we are bringing current fashion trends and wearable designs to the hand knitting industry. Hearing all of your feedback and reactions to our collections is what drives and shapes Quail Studio. We thank you for joining us on our journey.

Finally, we must thank all of the team at Rowan for supporting our publications, and working with us to create designs we are proud of, in a vast array of beautiful yarns.